THE MAP IS NOT THE TERRITORY

Poems and Selected Translations - 1972-1989

Dennis Maloney

UNICORN PRESS

Acknowledgements

Some of these poems and translations have appeared in the following periodicals: *Bloomsbury Review, Buffalo Gnats, Blue Jacket, Arachne, The Margarine Maypole Orangoutang Express, Adirondack Almanack, Slipstream, Niagara Magazine, INC., Jimson Weed, Buckle, Uroboros, Nomad, Pure Light, Cutting Edge, Wood Ibis, Ironwood, Aevum, Intrepid, Willow Springs, High Rock Review, CV II, The Buffalo News, Black Mountain II Review, Alternative Press, Articles, The Monthly Planet, Survivor, Grapevine, Plucked Chicken, Beyond Our Control, Buffalo Arts Review, Earth's Daughters, American Poetry Review, Yellow Silk,* and in the anthologies *Bear Crossings* and the *Buffalo Book of Poetry.*

Many of these poems and translations have also appeared in the following books: *Wanderings* (Bear Print, 1974), *Rimrock* (White Pine Press, 1978), *I Learn Only To Be Contented* (Raiyu Press, 1981), *Return* (White Pine Press, 1983), *Pine Hut Poems* (Swift Kick Press, 1984), *Sitting In Circles* (Blue Jacket Press, 1987), *Dusk Lingers*: Issa (White Pine Press, 1981), *Windows That Open Inward*: Pablo Neruda (White Pine Press, 1985), *The Landscape Of Soria*: Antonio Machado (White Pine Press, 1985), *The Stones Of Chile*: Pablo Neruda (White Pine Press, 1986), *Tangled Hair*: Yosano Akiko (White Pine Press, 1986), and *Light And Shadows*: Juan Ramon Jimenez (White Pine Press, 1987)

The author would like to thank the Witter Bynner Foundation for Poetry, the New York State Council on the Arts, and Erie County for grants which provided encouragement and support during the work on some of these poems and translations.

Publication of this book was made possible, in part, by a grant from the North Carolina Arts Council.

ISBN 0-87775-231-1 (paper)
ISBN 0-87775-232-x (cloth)

Unicorn Press, Inc.
P.O. Box 3307
Greensboro, N.C. 27402

For Elaine

CAMINANTE, NO HAY CAMINO
SE HACE CAMINO AL ANDAR.

TRAVELER, THERE IS NO ROAD
YOU MAKE YOUR OWN PATH AS YOU WALK.

—ANTONIO MACHADO

CONTENTS

I

II

III

THE MAP IS NOT THE TERRITORY

I

RETURN

The weather has cleared
and swiftly moving masses
of clouds obscure
and reveal a struggling sun.

The first scarlet tinges
set flame to the hills.
How foolish the time
spent in the city
worrying over the clutter
of events that fill our days.

Here I return to listen
to the stones and the wind.
With each gust
a thousand conversations begin.
Only the whine of a speedboat
on the river breaks this calm.

For an hour of the afternoon
I have watched a pair
of red tail hawks
follow roads out over the air
into countries we know nothing of.

Then in a quiet moment they
burst back through the trees
brushing their wings roughly
against the leaves
startled by a return
to the world that we know.

RIMROCK

We came here
to live with the rock.
Fashioned a hut
with vague rooms
of sky, tree and earth.
Gathering enough wood
to last the night.

After dusk
drawn near the fire
with Keith and Lisa
I watch the first stars
fill our ceiling
with silence.

SPRINGTIME RIMROCK

On the edge of the mountain
legs tucked up under
and pressed against rock.

The wind reaches
deep into the ear
with its music.

A sparrow hawk
flaps out
soaring high over the river
gliding gently out of sight
into the brown hills
which are just now
bursting into green.

SUNSET

Perched on a rock
watching the red ball
now a blazing sun
slip slowly
behind miles of green hills.

Dusk settles in the valley
waiting for the moon.

A moon reflected
in the river below
as waves of light.

Stumbling a narrow path
through the dark,
leaves of mountain laurel
gleam in the lantern light.

IN THE VOICE OF THUNDER,
THE RUSH OF RAIN

Caught up in a cleft,
a cave in the rock
we watch a storm rise.
The dark cloud sky body
that curls up
as it crosses the valley
flailing fistfuls of rain
down on us.

He-no spirit of rain
magic feather in hair
sends vajra diamond lightning bolts
flashing across the sky,
riding the dark cloud formations.

Leaving the sparkling nets of vapor
to float in the air,
pink and white petals of
mountain laurel
scattered in tiny pools,
the whole watershed coming alive.

TRILLIUM

At the base of a tree
near the cabin porch
among tufts of new spring grass
glistening in the rain
weaving in the wind
a single white trillium
petals unfolding in the new light

A POEM FOR MUSKRAT

Years of crisscrossing these hills
sleeping in holes in the ground
you sit on a half-rotted log
or amble about nosing garbage cans
near the cabin
fat belly scraping the ground

Till the sudden screech
smell of rubber
speed along new asphalt thruway
sends your plump body sailing
to land dead by the side of the road

Air is now your resting place

THE CABIN

Three days of spring rain
two weeks back from Japan
returning to this land

You getting washed
half-naked by the pump
in the cool evening

We drink glasses of wine
in praise of the stars
A mouse slips under the door
Moth wings beat against windowpanes
Making love into the night
Rain drumming the roof

BY THE SIDE OF RED HOUSE LAKE

Birds sing a last song.

The firs   the maples
the mountains darken.
Dissolving into the lake.

As if
they were never really there
only dark.

Suddenly a fish
breaks the surface. . .

HEALING THE WOUND

I walk down
an old logging road
toward the river.
Patches of gravel
barely show
through the carpet
of Queen Anne's lace
and other mountain grasses.
Bits of iron guardrail
here and there rust
back into the earth.
Soon the maples and birch
will sprout saplings
and the forest will
close back up on itself.
Healing the wound.

HEARTS CONTENT

Twelve miles of rough road
have brought me here
where a remnant of
the planet remains
spared from the logger's ax.

A forested place
dark, moist, quiet
without the remarkable vistas
which draw crowds to a spot.

Few find the way
and even fewer stay.
A family arrives by car.
Without stopping the engine
the father announces
"There's nothing here
just a bunch of trees"
and they drive off.

There is a silence here.
The silence of trees
who have sat
with straight spines
like Buddhist meditators
breathing and listening
for hundreds of years.
Bluejays and woodpeckers
weave songs in their crowns.
Chipmunk twitter
about the roots.

The trees which die
lie where they have fallen
untouched by the blade
of the woodsman's saw.
Becoming the detritus feast
of lichen, moss and
those tiny patient fungi
who take a century
to digest a single trunk.

A STAND OF PINES

How unlike nature's
random acts
of beauty and design
is this forest stand
of Red Pines planted
eight foot on center
in each direction
for acres and acres
by men of little
other possibility
in the depression years.

No sun penetrates
the dense crown.
Walking through
at mid-day, it is like
the midnight sky
without stars
and without shadow.
Trees so jammed together
the branches are dead
halfway to the top,
underneath, a mat of pine needles
where nothing grows.

THE CAMPFIRE

A humble beginning
of crumpled paper
and twig placed upon twig
created the spacious rooms
of this brilliant mansion.
The lower floor glows
with a golden orange
of longing, steady and intense
and yellow flames race
through the upper floors
like the sparks of
a young man's desire.
Consuming itself,
all is reduced
rooms, joy, and desires
to a bed of black coals
upon which I set
a pot of water to boil.

FOREST SPRING

Tiny spring bubbling forth
in the diffuse evening light
your gurgling voice
brings my mind to rest.
I drink from your stream
only half of what
my hands will hold
and return the remainder
to continue the gift.
Tiny spring forever giving
with no thought of return,
source we hold precious,
without you our lives
are so much less.

This morning I return
once more to drink
from your stream.
I sit on a boulder above
listening
and the rest of the world
has enough sense
to leave us alone.
Morning light finds paths
through the branches above.

WHITE PINE

The rider riddle is easy to ask,
but the answer might surprise you.

                    -Lew Welch

1

Five long needles
soft to the touch
when brushed against
hand or face
the resinous scent
of pitch
stuck to the fingers
lingers still

2

White pine
is
imperfect
snow
completes
it

3

"Untrainable"
the bonsai expert
said

15

red pine, scots pine,
hemlock
can be bent, formed
and shaped
but not that
"white pine"

4

In this place
I plant the tree of the great peace
under the shade
of the great white pine
we sit
on soft white cushions
of thistledown
roots spread
in all directions

5

Cities
you
kill me
with your
chemical air
choke my tissues
turn my needles
brown

drive me
from my place
I cannot even
die
gracefully

6

Hearts Content, Pennsylvania
the loggers' apology
for the destruction
of the white pine forests
of New York and Pennsylvania
twenty acres
of virgin biotic
intelligence
left
like it was
before

7

Wine bottle
in hand
drunk again
we do
the dance of
the trembling pine
in the breeze

8

White pine
what was
given me
to ride
by
the sweet lady
who sang me
these songs
whispered to
the heart

The mysteries
constantly revealed
seldom understood

9

We are
the people
of the white pine

We dance
as the wind
moves thru us

We praise
the sunlight
falling heavy

on our branches

We are patient
and live o'
a long time
a long time

II

My hut lies in the middle of a dense forest;
Every year the green ivy grows longer.
No news of the affairs of men,
Only the occasional song of a woodcutter.
The sun shines and I mend my robe;
When the moon comes out I read Buddhist poems.
I have nothing to report, my friends.
If you want to find the meaning, stop chasing after
so many things.

—Ryokan

PINE HUT POEMS

1

Pine hut hermitage
like the dwellings
of those few before
A place to rest
this bag of bones
we call human

On the road
it travels with him
the boundaries
his own heart
the landscape traversed
the full moon overhead

2

Out the window
snow lines the
neighboring roofs

Occasional flakes
drift in the air
Spring Equinox morning

3

After late April snow
suddenly it's spring

as he strides out
from the house
into the warm afternoon

Yellow forsythias
catch the eye

4

Today
the tractor sits
silent, ignored
Barn swallows
twittering under
pale grey rafters

Beer keg in the yard
While upstairs
strains of bluegrass
fill the room

Planting done
men and women
delight
making music

5

Two poets
cruise the roads
surveying the new fields

like a couple of crows
mapping out the summer's feast
chanting

        corn corn
        wheat wheat
        corn corn

6

The rush
from the view
of water
falling
not enough
for the
engineering students
who stand
attempting to
calculate
velocity and flow

7

He peers at the moss
between knobby roots

A soft green forest
through which animals
quietly move

8

The fledging robin
didn't even notice
the cat
whose owner
was just
ever so late
to intercede

Buried beneath
the lilac
it will live
in next year's
flowers

9

This morning
as he rose
to go out
to weed the garden
a slice of moon
lingered

Dew clinging
to grasses

10

He recalls
a day years ago
making love at dawn
the Summer Solstice

Hidden behind dense yews
their shapes remained
imprinted on the grass

11

Brief shower
smell of
sweet summer grasses

The poet
abandons himself
to the joys
that surround him

12

On a night
like any other
the persistent voice
of a cricket
punctuates
hot stillness

13

Miles before it arrives
rain announces itself
Long rumblings
and brief flashes
in the evening sky

Wood smoke
flames lick
the edges
of a shake

A solitary man
sits at the table
writing by
lantern light

In the middle
of the night
rain drops drum
taut tent canvas

14

Watering the garden
at twilight
deep soak to roots

tomatoes set, fruit formed
sweet peppers ready to flower

Among the crackle of fireworks
this fourth of July
his thoughts turn
to the Seneca women
who tilled this ground
before him
happy for promises
the earth held

As he recoils the hose
the arc of a roman candle
lights up the sky

15

Taking notice
he steps over
a single
tomato plant
nurtured by
car exhaust

Existence precarious
in a crack between
curb and walk
Casting a shadow
heavy with
three green fruit

16

Behind the house
long rows of
tomato
squash
pumpkin
radish
pepper
cabbage
bean
overgrown
with green shoots of
morning glories
twined and looping
around the plants
A harvest of
pink, purple, blue
bell-shaped flowers
for the eye

17

Her dark hair
spills over the pillow
and across her shoulder
long strands
tangle in his mouth
as they make love

Later she traces
the lines of his palm
roads he will follow

18

The morning
full of bird songs

When one
would be enough

19

How hard
it is to
follow the course
the lifestream takes

To speak of

going with
caught up in

the flow

Balancing that
act of
resistance
Rock in midstream
finally worn down

washed away

20

Late at night
he arrives
entering the cottage
by a door
left slightly ajar
quietly treading the floor
he finds a place of rest
in the dim light

Next to the bed
a welcome of
cheese, bread and wine

21

He returns home
after a long journey
The grass overgrown
curves back on itself
and the garden shows
obvious neglect

Piles of
unanswered mail
clutter the desk

22

Poet, painter
sit quiet
and listen

The lines, the words
and their music
must flow from the heart

It is best to sweep
the mind clean
and be left
with a blank page

23

He takes from the forest
only what is given

the pines, the hemlocks
a tangle of hardwoods
the clear spring
and the woman
who walks paths
with him through
this ancient grove

They rest on boulders
above the spring
before gathering up

the children
a few twigs and cones

They turn homeward

24

At thirty
you worry of aging
Yes we age
grow old
but we will
do so with
an ease
and grace as
the cherry tree
at Maruyama Park
which never fails
each year to blossom
gorgeous
Elegant as
Tu Fu's beard
Tara's eternal smile

25

Sitting in circles
centered on the fire
surrounded by friends
he reads poems aloud
by lantern light

The words escape
into the black night
and we are drawn
into flame
and out to
shadowy trees
and the gleaming
jeweled net
of evening stars

26

The children
brought you
handfuls
of wildflowers
A vase of which now graces
the kitchen table

Two days later
a killing frost
Summer remains
in the purple
and yellow bouquet

27

After a long autumn
he dances in the field
near his hut

The first flakes
of snow swirling
around him at evening

28

Having addressed
the tasks
of his day

morning in meditation
afternoon well-spent
writing friends
dinner complete
floor swept
dishes washed
he steps out into crisp air

29

At his writing desk
he watches
snow articulate
the interlacing tangle
of branches
Late afternoon
fading into dusk

30

Caught in a storm
the full blade
of wind
cuts to the bone

Slogging streets
snow pelts his face
freezing to his beard
peering
peering
the eye can
scarcely discern
the path home

31

Spirit sore
he walks
with the pain
of the one
who is gone
and the emptiness
of the one
left behind

32

Evening of
the Winter Solstice

crushing dry herbs
fragrant harvest
consumes the room

33

He shuts the door
secure against the storm
boils water for tea
and lights a stick of incense

At his writing desk
or sitting back
in the chair reading
he thinks occasionally
of friends separated
by miles and the snow
and smiles to himself

34

Lifting shovel after shovel
he hardly notices the city
watching more flakes
settle down

Later out the back window
he studies how to trim back
the bare branches of
a huge silver maple

Where to stake out
the vegetable garden
favoring a sunny spot
raspberries and strawberries
to be planted
along the fence
wildflowers and dogwood
in the shade
compost heap to be started
first thing in the spring

NANZEN-JI

Climbing the hills
behind Nanzen-ji
in a light rain

Past the aqueduct
and the old Buddhist cemetery
trails of slick rock and mud

The old Dharma paths
crisscrossing and twining
folding into the cedars

There is no end

The gong sends
a deep voice following
the face of the hill
up

SHISEN-DO

Tired of fighting
Jozan Ishikawa
quit the world and
built his hermitage
at the foot of Higashiyama

Did you think
clipped azaleas
white sand
a view of the moon
would be enough?

Listening to the clacking water gong
against rock all night long
writing poems

In spring azaleas will bloom again
but now it's snowing
and I'm cold and alone

GINKAKU-JI

Temple of
the silver pavilion

not really silver

Ah, but on the night
of the full moon

DAITOKU-JI

Fallen pink petals
in a neat circle
around the base
of the camellia tree
Another promise of yesterday

CHOIN-IN

In the Hojo
monks intone
NAMU AMIDA BUTSU
a thousand times
to the clack
of the wooden fish drum

MYOSHIN-JI

Myoshin-ji compound
The main temple and forty sub-temples
appearing one at a time
thru openings in the high clay walls
huge wooden doors pulled aside
We wander inside the gate
look around the front garden
and meet a monk going out for the mail

He wonders
who are these foreigners
who don't know enough Japanese
to ask where the garden is
and what do they want?

Without question
the old monk
leads us to a gate
just beyond the garden
along a stone path
and up a small rise
to the grave of an ancient roshi
His profile etched in stone
thin with years of wandering
walking stick and traveler's hat
enlightened smile
at having made it
to the other shore
and back
returning again
to guide us
to this place

KITANO SHRINE

Here for the fair
buying brown bread
bag of mandarin oranges
searching out a tea set
with plum blossom design

A man straps
the rootball of
a cherry sapling
to the luggage rack
of his bicycle
and pedals away

A few blossoms
gently sway overhead

KU-TEI

I learn only to be contented.

The stone basin rim
holds the pool
whose water
the ancient mirror
shines.

The bamboo shadows
sweep the stairs
but raise no dust.

The mirror
is the voice
which has no sound
but is clearly heard.

And this place,
the place
where we are now
Ku-tei
the garden of emptiness.

IN HEIAN STYLE
for Taeko Takaori

Passing through
the garden gate
noise of traffic
drops away

We stroll
your father's garden
with childhood stories,
playing in the stream
with your brother
watching father
create the garden

Lanterns from China
stones brought down
from the mountains
by horsecart

Digging the stream,
rarranging rocks
till the ripple
of water is right

Banks of Bamboo and Sasa,
mounds of azaleas,
the mottled bark
of lacebark pine
planted in a pair

We feed the multicolor carp
composing poems
along the path
and follow stepping stones
to the tea house
where we sip powdered green tea
from fine warm bowls
in Heian style

KOTO-IN

Above broom-swept ground
tight new maple buds
unfold delicate leaves
enjoyed with no thought
of autumn

LOOKING FOR LUNCH

Walking through Kanazawa streets
with a Shinto priest's son
encountering
Cleancut American Mormon Missionary Boys
hustling Bibles to the natives
noticing my long locks they say
"You look like a samurai"

All praise to Manjusri
Bodhisattva of Wisdom
blue-eyed red-lipped
who rides the lion
carries in his hand
The Prajna Paramita Heart Sutra
that he may instruct, cutting away
Ignorance and Delusion with
his Diamond Vajra Sword

MT. ASO FOOTHILLS

Low peaks snow covered
High peaks lost in fog
Cold morning air

By the roadside
second growth hinoki
sugi
hand-cut

Branches trimmed
from straight spines
tied in bundles
or burned to warm

Trunks lashed
to the pickup
the old man and wife
drive off

IN KYUSHU:
WATCHING THE SUNSET FROM A TRAIN

Two men lifting
shovelsful of dirt
from ditch to
wheelbarrow

Further
a farmer
his wife
spreading hay

A schoolgirl
in black
riding her bike
Another

walking beside
down a dirt road

YAMAUBA

Behold
she who was here
a while ago

Yamauba Yamauba

Now
is no more
to be seen
anywhere

Yamauba Yamauba

She who flies over mountains
voice echoing
up and down
the valleys

Yamauba Yamauba

Forever
from mountain to mountain
wandering wandering

Yamauba Yamauba

She has vanished now
into the land
of nowhere

Yamauba Yamauba Yamauba

MIYAJIMA

Tall old pines
lean out
toward the bay
listening

HIGASHI HONGAN-JI

Under the huge wooden roof
walking toward the Amida Buddha
the smell of new mats

TOKYO DAWN

Houses, gardens
filled with
the dusty silence
of dawn
Broken by
the caw of
a large black crow
sweeping the dirty sky

OUT A TRAIN WINDOW

Fat crows
pluck at hard earth
in a light snow
and fly off
out of sight

LIVING ALONE

Living alone
in this space
between the rocks
far from the city
Here,
where no one can see
I shall give myself away

OUT OF THE DARK

Out of the dark
from along the canal
the steady slow beat
from the hide-covered drum
of three begging monks.

TODAI-JI

Walk through the awesome wooden gate
And up the stone steps
Under the enormous Daibutsu-den roof
The huge statue of Vairocana
Daibutsu of Avatamsaka
Buddha of the Great Illumination

Says the booklet:

Body	:53.3 feet high, seated on Lotus
Face	:16 feet high, 9.5 feet wide
Eye	:3.9 feet wide
Nose	:1.6 feet
Ear	:8.5 feet
Thumb	:4.8

His hands shaping
The mudra: "Do not fear"

Sudden translation,
            that reassuring voice:
"You're in good hands with Buddha"

That giant hand
Outstreached
To protect

LOOKING DOWN ON KYOTO

Sunday afternoon walk
Along the eastern hills
I follow a canal
North from Nanzen-ji
Looking for Shisen-do
Get lost and find instead
Rough hewn stone steps
Leading to the top of the mountain
Where Shinto priests
In bright robes and badger pelts
Performing ritual
Offer us sake
In praise of Tanuki
The big bellied badger
Under a wide traveler's hat
Grinning with sagging balls
Jug of sake in one paw
A cup in the other

Looking back down on Kyoto
Catching a glimpse, a vision of the city
As seen a few days before
At San-ju-san-gen-do:
Senju-Kwannon
Thousand armed
The hands holding
Bells, wands, flowers, a factory,
Mountains, waterfalls,
Vajra thunderbolts, lovers, flags,
Daggers, the Sanjo street bridge,
Streetcars, tiny stone gardens,

Coffeehouses, bars, shops,
A grid of streets, prayer beads,
The textile looms of Nishijin,
Toyota taxi, vases, ancient temples,
High rise apartment buildings,
Conch shell trumpets, the Bullet Express,
A fistfull of snow, rice paddies,
Books, bottles, Dharma wheels,
The wash under the eaves,
All happening in a wink
Or a laugh

How can that old woman
With her walking stick
Climb this slope with such ease
when my legs are sore
And I'm out of breath

IV

AT FIRST LIGHT

Turning over
at first light
streaming in
between curtains
my fingers reach out
caress shoulder,
cup breast,
stroke belly

Both of us
still damp
after a night
of lovemaking.

LOOKING AT PHOTOGRAPHS

You showed me
a photo of yourself
revealing
only a portion

Tough eyes
a characteristic
thrust of the head
That don't mess
with me look

But another
caught you softer
and smiling

Still another pose
reflected only in
your lover's eyes

A face
full of wildness
as a mare
galloping across
an open field
Ecstatic brilliant eyes
dazzled on
the verge of climax

AT DAWN

Not wanting to rise
into the cold
but content
to lie beneath
the warm covers
snuggled against you
till necessity
obliges me
to take leave
ever so gently

Out from the house
braced with tea
for the road
I proceed
watching the dark blue
night sky fade
into the unfolding dawn

In the hollow places
frost has covered
the grasses
greeting the morning
this morning

A SUMMER DANCE

There is pleasure
in each touch
and glance

Moonlight on the river
The dripping coolness
of a summer shower

The whirl and
mad abandon
in every rock and roll dance

And the brilliance
of the sun
transformed
in the dark
curves of your
flesh caressed

AN ATTRACTION

Through smoke
the scent of you
not musk or
another perfume

A subtle essence
that allures
and thus
enchants

FRIEND, LOVER

The tendency
is to say my
as in my woman
though this
is not entirely accurate
as I disdain
the possessive implied
in that
suggesting something
less than whole

Better perhaps
to say friend
or lover
to define
our separate selves

Though there are
those moments
when two
become one

BEHIND BLUE EYES

Leaning on the space heater
cradled in each other's arms
we soon find ourselves
in bed in the other room

In the candle flicker
and incense smoke
we explore the topography
with first tentative
then sure movements

Beyond soft belly folds
my hand reaches to
your moist place
massaging with
our own essetial oils
tasting the pleasures
of the harbor

Behind blue eyes
Celtic mind
intunes the patterns
which connect ourselves
to self
and each other
and the ground
we dance upon
at morning tangled
limbs entwined

THE FEVER

You phoned delirious
asking would I come.
So I drove the hour and a half
through winter
to your apartment.

Curled up on the couch
you wake in occasional fits
between long periods of sleep.

I am able to provide little
except for the simplest
of acts.
A glass of ice water
pressed to your dry lips.
Perhaps my presence alone
is some comfort,
a solace
to see you through.

I focus on the
shifting clouds
of sunset
between reading
and listening
to the rise and fall
of congested breath
fill the hours.

By morning
the fever has broken

and you acknowledge
the world again,
surprised I'm here,
not remembering
you'd called.

WINTER ALBA

Morning, too soon
sunlight bright
through the windows

The bed warm
wrapped each
in the other
we wake from
a common dream

Out into a
bitter cold
scrape the car windows
and begin
our separate days

V

LETTER TO THE EDITOR

To whom it may concern:
If possible
I would appreciate
some information
about getting published.
I have been writing poetry
since nine,
I am now 25.
I feel it is time
to make my work available
to as many people
that need
and can appreciate it.
My writing as you shall see
is truly a gift from god
and touches each person
that reads it.

I have poems
all shapes and sizes
about everything possible
each with its own
seed planting message.
I do not consider it religious
poetry in society's sense.
Yet is life not religion?
I assure you it would be
to your advantage to reply
as you shall see once you read my work.

WHO ARE THE HEROES

Mid-November. I walk through the square, across the grass tinged white. A dusting of snow settles on the gold and crimson leaves. They will be pressed to the ground beneath the sodden weight all winter till they become transparent nets of veins giving what little they hold back to the earth.

In the center of the square stands the statue of a now forgotten Civil War general, mounted on horse prepared to charge into battle. Across the stone pedestal someone has scrawled with black paint "the peace makers are the heroes."

Here the general sits, eyes alert, spurs digging into the flanks of his horse. He carries a sword raised above his head, leading the charge, plunging into battle. Into the shouts and crys, the gunsmoke, and blood. What was that last thought as the bullet pierced your flesh?

The boy of twelve or fourteen receives a gun from his father and gives up playing. He walks down a country road alone, gun slung over his shoulder. A gold finger ring lost for centuries is found among the ruins. On it the goddess stands at a small shrine, bare breasted, between two men; one is tearing out a tree by the roots, the other kneels weeping.

A PLACE NOT EASILY FILLED

I remember my first visit to this supermarket after moving into the neighborhood. I was still hung over from too many farewell rounds the night before. Even hung over I marveled at the wood floors. Wood floors I thought! When was the last time I'd seen wood floors in a supermarket? Floors of character, varnish worn off, with scrapes and scars showing the years.

Buying a few necessities, I returned to the pile of cartons and furniture that would gradually begin to resemble a home.

I didn't know you well, only one among the several who checked out my groceries and with whom I exchanged coin and pleasantry. You became visibly pregnant along with the coming spring and with the slow arrival of summer, took leave to give birth. I never gave a thought as to your return. But one day you were suddenly there at the register ringing up soap and beer, making change, as before.

Not long after, returning from a weekend out of town, I stopped by the store to pick up some groceries and found it strangely closed. The TV news that evening held the answer. Two young men had entered the store that morning bent on robbery and made their way to the office demanding money with the revolver drawn. You gave them all there was, yet they let a bullet fly as they fled. It pierced your body, your young body which had so recently blossomed.

The words of your death exploded in my stomach as if the bullet had ripped through me. It was a week before I could enter the store, filled with a hollowness, a place not easily filled.

DAWN IN VERONA

in memory of James Wright

Near dawn I arrive in this city you so loved and adopted as
your home late in life, far from your native Ohio. The night has been
passed in the uncomfortable sleep of a train berth. As the morning
opens I step down from the train surrounded by the soft chatter of
another language I do not understand settling on my ears like a dusty
fog, clouds of mist which partly engulf the adjacent olive trees and
houses.

Waiting for the connecting train, which is characteristically
late, I think of you, briefly, this morning, and of your love for the
Adige River and how you discovered the secret of its light. I board the
train and slouch into its hardwood seats, the light falling on the empty
railway platform changing character moment by moment.

Perhaps you are here now sitting in a tiny garden waiting for
the strong morning sun to arrive and burn off the fog. Clouds of fog
like the grief you sometimes felt for the heart of an America dark as the
mud at the bottom of the Ohio River. The train pulls out headed for
another city.

SUFI BASEBALL

Four yellow butterflies
dance around homeplate
like dervishes
Are they
the batter, the catcher
the ump and the coach
arguing
                or is it
that the batter has
hit a grand slam homer
and is just about to
tag home and be congratulated
by his excited teammates
and the wind in the grass
is the fans in the stands
gone wild
                or is it
that a runner is sliding
into home and
the pitcher has moved in
to cover the plate
while the catcher
fields the overthrown ball
and the ump stands
waiting to make the call
                or is it
that four yellow butterflies
are whirling about homeplate
on an otherwise
deserted diamond

THE TREASURES

Turned-brown faded picture
of a small girl smiling.

A white spruce
roots, trunk, limbs and branch
tied in small bundles
with scent still.
The man said
      "Got too big for the house"

An old kerosene stove, rusty but workable.

A black diary the only entry:
      "On this 7th day of January
       In the year of our Lord 1955
       I found out that
       Jean liked someone else."

Things that no longer fit
left out with the trash.

STAKEOUT THE TERRAIN

Survey and stakeout the terrain
with rod and transit
on a morning of late winter .
Near the center of the city
the crumbling of decay
and urban renewal create
huge vacancies in the landscape.
Neighborhoods slip into history
eaten away by the mouths of bulldozers.
This air of vacancy surrounds
four 19th century brick houses
that remain on an otherwise empty street.
Wind rattles the broken windows.

Survey and stake out a field nearby
with transit and rod,
the measure of a space
full of last year's weeds,
and remnants of snow,
and sections of newspaper
decomposing stories and events
back into earth and memory.
Unlike the scattered styrofoam
hamburger containers
which last forever.

OFFICE WORK

It is a hot summer afternoon
and we are in the air conditioned office
drafting lines on paper.
Two-dimensional representations of space
that transformed will be a park
with trees, grass, and benches
months from now.
But we tire of drawing lines
and want now to be
in some other version of reality.
Perhaps the park itself
feeling the sun on our shoulders
or the shade of a tree.
Or on some tropical beach
with warm sea breeze and beer
far away from the air conditioning,
desk and traffic.
Or hiking in a cool hemlock woods
without phones and appointments
except those we make
with the silent part of ourselves.

LISTENING TO THE PAUL WINTER CONSORT

In the two hundred year old
shaker chapel
a symbiotic dialog
of sea, land and sky beings
joined in swirling conversations
of pure mammal music

Bats glide
between rafters
and dive out
open windows into
the black night

Much as we
dive beneath
the surface of
luminous oceans
of sound
and listen to
humpback whales
weave songs
over distance
to each other

As the masks
of personality
slip away
we are all
emanations of a
larger note

FOOTSTEPS

Footsteps. Footsteps.
About seven in the evening
is the time they came.

We sat in our huts
listening for
the footsteps, footsteps.

They drove us from
our cities and towns
like cattle.
The merchants are gone,
the square is empty.
No longer do the voices
of children rise
from the alleys.

Into the country
we were driven
as slaves to labor
in the fields.
After every planting
and every harvest
they would come again
because we weren't needed.

We sat in our huts
listening, listening
for the footsteps.
One by one
a sister, a brother

a husband, a father
a cousin, a child
disappeared into the night.

She calls to her dog
which comes and
curls up at her feet.
This is what I have left
for a family now.

ON THE ANNIVERSARY OF
MARTIN LUTHER KING JR.'S BIRTHDAY

The demonstration
for anger and hate
by a lone neo-nazi
is not part of
this remembrance
      Nor
is the empty rhetoric
of our counter marches
      Or
the faces of
politely smiling politicians
all gathered
in the spotlight of
the assembled media

To those who join
in the peace
let them celebrate
the memory of the day
and recognize
in each man and woman
the only measure

The person and
the actions
extending from that

ACROSS FROM WASHINGTON SQUARE PARK

Six pines,
one dead
grow in a
Japanese manner
angled towards the sun
or what light
there is
reflected from surfaces
various as
the light itself

An exercise
in breath
reaching to
the space and air
of the square
across the street

A BROKEN BRANCH

A splintered branch
without leaf or bark,
rattling its empty song
in the wind.
Year after year
tired of living
and dying,
its song tenacious,
hiding fear.
Another winter,
another spring.

VI

HERMIT OF THE DUNES

He lives alone
in this insubstantial landscape
of sand, wind
and salt breeze.
Like the tough sea grasses
he clings to the slope
living in a vacant squatter's shack.
An empty shell made home,
like the crabs that burrow
below the sand at low tide
on the tidal pools
of the harbor.

He has rebuilt his shack
five or six times on top of itself
as year after year
the blowing, shifting sand
has gradually filled
the room below.
Here he lives
with a few simple things
tools, cooking pot, books.

Seldom seen in town,
during winter kind strangers
leave food at his door.
Occasionally someone spots him
at night walking alone
on the dunes
in his solitude
his white beard glowing
in the moonlight.

MORNING IN PLAYA DORADA

We breakfast
and the local blackbirds do too.
My companion insists the greeting
they sing each morning is 'buenos dias'.
The locals call the bird Chinchilin,
slender and intensely black
from feet to beak, they flit about
feasting on crumbs.

An unfamiliar landscape,
above and far beyond the birds,
the palm and banana trees
is a small mountain
whose ragged outline
disappears and reappears
in the mist and rain
of the morning.
Patches of light green
contrast those of dark
and the lines of horse trails
lead back into the mountain
where marginal farmers
scratch out a meager life.

Morning mist clouds the mountain
in an iridescent light
until suddenly it disappears completely.

The natives waiting on us
and cleaning the tables
pretend to love us
and perhaps do
in their own ambiguous way.
The blackbirds bluster about
in couples performing
a mating dance not for us,
the attentive public,
but for themselves.

AFTER HEARING KENNETH REXROTH READ

Strolling the park path
in the distance
trees of magnolia buds
reflecting moonlight

A little closer
and suddenly
we are surrounded
by the presence
of marvelous beings
whose scent perfumes
the adjacent atmosphere

In Kyoto now
the cherry blossoms
have opened and the population
responds with singing
dancing and carrying on
making friends
under the boughs

But here we are alone
among these trees
whose leaf buds
are still curled up
tight against the cold
in the midst
of Highland Park
overlooking city lights

Is there no one else
to share
this joy?

TO THE GODDESS OF DAWN IN PRAISE

Shivering
in a wet sleeping bag
the whole night long
through the rain.

To wake at dawn
to the smell of damp cedar.

A heron crying
through the mist
off the lake.

A SONG FOR TOM

A rainy Tuesday
in May and
you have died
passing through
the membrane
which separates
this world
from the next

The music of your
mountain hammer dulcimer
resonated like the rain
among the hollows
and fields of this
lake plain geography
gathering full
in the lush, liquid
chambers of each
grape upon the vine

Our inheritance
the humor
and quiet strength
which marked
the passage
of your ordeal

Tom, the grief
is larger
with one so young
but know friend

you will be remembered
in the voices
of children
you taught to sing
and in those
moments of memory
etched upon
the uncarved block

SQUARE DANCING AT THE TOWN HALL

The release
and exuberance
swinging your
partner
to and fro
to and fro
melts the
body's chill
this frigid night

The caller
chimes the tune
and the fiddler
joins in

Circle to the left
then circle
to the right
wheel to the left
then wheel
to the right
and circle on back

Swing your partner
do see do
changing partners
all night long
till happy
and exhausted
we promenade
on home

CHANDA'S PLACE

Beaming with pride
you just had
to show us
and we followed
the flashlight beam
into the dark yard
to your clubhouse
Crafted joist
to sill to lintel
as a full size house
would be

The incense of new wood
fills the space inside
Your place now
an expression of love
from your father's skilled hands

All winter long as now
the sagging branches
of the Norway Spruce
will cast shadows
in the moonlight above

NIGHT SKY

Driving north
we are surrounded
by huge masses
of vegetative shadow.

The subtle hues
of dark blue swirls
and clumps of clouds
illuminated by a
hidden moon
entertain my eyes
not a star in sight.

Further along
a city of lights
draws us in
houses hugging hills
down the valley.

POINT REYES PENINSULA

In the hot September air
the hills covered
with stubby shrubs
and brown burnt grass

The only trees
define human settlement
and herds of cows
graze on straw
strewn in long paths
over the round hills
falling gently
toward the sea

At night ghost Tule Elk
range unfettered

SWIMMING IN THE GENESEE

Under sheer canyon cliffs
walls worn smooth
by centuries of flow

We flow too
with this stream
slipping over algae covered rock

Stroking into a deep pool
the current streams
in, around and through us

Horseplaying we smear
each others bodies
with mud

And later listen to
tiny waterfall music
cleanse our ears

As we stretch out
bare to dry
on the shale bank

Overhead a band of hawks
swoop and dip
swoop and dip

WHITEFACE MOUNTAIN

Thin mantle of soil
Building up, building up
Lichens cracking rock
Moss filling the depressions
Holding soil.
Mountain sandwort
Flowers all summer long
Becomes humus
Enriching next year's blossoms.

The plants here
Are small and tough
Standing strong
Against this harsh climate.
Beautiful alpine gardens
Of tiny bearberry willow
And three tooth cinquefoil.
Near the leeward side
Of the summit
Hundred year old Balsam Firs
Six feet high
Stand like flags
Pointing the direction
Of the wind.

ON BULLY HILL

Sitting on the hillside veranda
Surrounded by vineyard in leaf
I gaze at Kueka Lake
A thousand feet below
Crystal as this glass
Of aurora blanc

Remembering each spring
The cutting back of dead growth
Tying and shaping each vine
Rooted in these shallow soils

Till sunlight grown heavy
We praise the harvest
Raising glass into the afternoon

Rumi says
"When grapes turn to wine
They long for our ability to change"

A ROUND FOR HIGHLAND PARK

Bedazzled
Our senses
Eyes bursting with color
Lilac bushes
Fill the slope
Clusters of cascading flowers
Several shades of purple, blue, white
(Genetic variation)

Bedazzled
The nose
Filled with fragrant scents
Each shade a different perfume
More delicate than the one before

A blossoming in playful delight
The music of soil and sunlight

SHALE ROCK UNDERFOOT

Shale rock underfoot
waves break around the feet
late September night breeze off lake

Fire already burning
soak corn in water
and place now
among the ash and coals

Take a last naked summer swim
in the chilly lake waters
as the corn slowly roasts

We each eat
two or three ears
washed down with beer

Build up the fire
and listen to a dulcimer song
blend with the rush of wave and wind
drinking in this moonlit lake night

AWAITING A REPLY

Day after day
no word or
letter arrives

Here the snow falls
with irregular frequency
The bitter cold
a constant companion
And on some nights
the howling wind
shakes the house

Tonight a glaze
of ice and
walking is
treacherous
Yet the adjacent lawns
are transformed
into facets of
a shimmering gem
by a nearby street lamp

How is your world?

VII

Translators are ghosts who live
in limbo between two worlds
the problem is not a question
of what gets lost in translation
but rather
what gets lost
between the happening of love or pain
and their coming into words.

for lovers or users of words
this is the difficulty -
what gets lost
is not what gets lost in translation but more
what gets lost in language itself.

Alastair Reid

POEMS OF ISSA

A warbler:
his muddy feet
wipe the plum blossoms

The cool breeze
makes its home
even in a blade of grass

In the cherry blossom's shade
complete strangers
do not exist

A spring day:
wherever there is water
dusk lingers

The mountain farmer
his hoe a pillow
skylarks singing

Tiny garden by the gate
just the thing:
this evening shower

A foot-high waterfall
splashes
cooling the evening

A bright full moon
my beat-up shack
is as you see it

POEMS OF YOSANO AKIKO

Pressing my breasts,
I gently part the veil of mystery.
Look! A flower
crimson and intense.

Near water, you slept at the great Saga Dam
love god of a single night.
The poem you composed within the silk bed,
please keep it secret.

Without speaking of the Way,
without worrying about the future,
without seeking fame,
here, loving, gazing at each other.

A thirsty lamb searching
the woods for water;
its eyes resemble yours,
my love!

Hair unbound from this hot house
of lovemaking scented with lilies
I dread the night
fading to pale rose.

Black hair,
tangled in a thousand strands,
tangled my hair and
tangled my thoughts and memories.

Poems of Antonio Machado
From THE LANDSCAPE OF SORIA

1.

The landscape of Soria is arid and cold.
Through the hills and barren mountains,
small green meadows, ashen hills,
spring passes
leaving among the fragrant grasses
tiny white daisies.

The earth doesn't revive, the fields sleep.
In early April snowfall covers
the back of Moncayo;
the traveler wraps his scarf
around his neck and mouth, and the
shepherds pass covered in their trailing capes.

II.

The tilled earth
like remnants of brown serge,
the small orchard, beehives, the bits
of dark green where sheep graze
between leaden, rocky slopes,
sow the joyful dream of a youthful Arcadia.
In the distant black poplars by the road
the stiff branches seem to smoke
with the blue-green mist of new leaves
and in the openings of valleys and ravines
the blackberry blossoms whiten
and the fragrant violets bloom.

IV.

Figures in the field against the sky!
A pair of oxen slowly plowing
a slope, as autumn begins,
and between the black heads
bent beneath the heavy yoke,
hangs a basket of rushes and broom;
a child's cradle.
Behind the team
a man plods, leaning towards the earth,
and a woman casts seed
into the open furrows.
Beneath a cloud of crimson and flame
in the fluid gold and green
of the west, the shadows grow huge.

V.

Snow. In an inn by an open field
you can see the hearth where wood smokes
and the kettle is bubbling and boiling.
The cold north wind sweeps over the motionless land,
exciting the silent snow
into white whirlwinds.
The snow settles on the fields and roads
as if on a grave.
An old man trembles and coughs, huddled
around the fire; an old woman spins
her twist of wool, and a girl sews
green trim on her scarlet cloth.

The old ones are parents of a muledriver
who journeyed over the white earth
one night, lost his way without a trace,
and was buried in the mountain snow.
Around the fire there is an empty place
and in the forehead of the old man, a sullen frown,
like a somber stroke,
from the blow of an ax on a log.
The old woman looks at the field, as if she hears
footsteps in the snow. No one passes.
The nearby road is empty
and the field surrounding the house deserted.
The girl is thinking of green meadows
where she will run with other girls
in the blue and golden days,
when the white daisies bloom.

VIII.

I have seen the golden poplars again,
roadside poplars along the banks
of the Duero, between San Polo and San Saturio,
beyond the old town walls
of Soria - by the outpost
towards Aragon, in Castile.

These black river poplars, that blend
the rustling of their dry leaves
with the sound of the river, when the wind blows,
have the initials and dates
of lovers

carved in their bark.

Poplars, of love, whose branches
were filled with nightingales yesterday,
poplars, that tomorrow will be lyres
of the fragrant spring wind,
love's poplars near the water
which flows, passes and dreams,
poplars on the banks of the Duero,
you along with me, my heart carries you!

IX.

Yes, you go with me, landscapes of Soria
calm afternoons, lavender mountains,
groves by the river, green dreams
of grey soil and brown earth,
aching melancholy
of the city's decay,
have you arrived in my soul
or were you already there in the depths?
People of the high plain
whom God watches over like old believers
may the Spanish sun fill you
with abundance, light, joy.

Poems of Pablo Neruda
SOLITUDES

Among the stones of the coast, walking,
by the shore of Chile,
farther off
sea and sea, moon and sea grass,
the lonely expanse of the planet.

The coast broken
by thunder,
consumed by the teeth of every dawn,
worn by great stirrings
of weather and waves:
slow birds circle,
with iron-colored feathers
and they know that here the world ends.
No one said why,
no one exists,
it isn't written, there are no numbers or letters,
no one trampled the obscure sand
like lead pollen:
here desolate flowers were born,
plants that expressed themselves with thorns
and sudden blossoms
of furious petals.
No one said there wasn't any territory,
that here the void begins,
the ancient emptiness that guides
with catastrophe, darkness
and shadow, darkness, shadows:
so it is the rough coast, that road
of south to north to west, to solitude.

Beautiful virtue, that of conflict,
that water and seafoam erect
along this long border:
the wave reconstructing itself like a flower,
repeating its castle-like form,
its tower that decays and crumbles
only to grow beating anew
like it sought
to populate the darkness with its beauty,
to fill the abyss with light.

Walking
from the final antarctic
by stone and sea, hardly
saying a word,
only the eyes speak and rest.

Innumerable solitude swept
by wind and salt, by cold,
by chains,
by moon and tides:
I must recall the toothless star
that here collapsed,
to gather the fragments
of stone, to hear
no one and speak with no one,
to be and not be a solitary motion of the heart:
I am the sentinel
of a barracks without soldiers,
of a great solitude filled with stones.

ODE TO A WOMAN GARDENER

Yes, I knew that your hands were
a gilliflower in bloom, the lily
of silver:
anything that had to do
with the soil,
with the blossoming of the earth,
but,
when
I saw you digging, digging,
removing small stones
and overcoming roots,
I suddenly knew,
my farmer,
that not only
your hands
but your heart
was of the earth,
that there
you understood
and made
things yours,
touching
moist
doors
through which
whirl
the seeds.

Thus, as,
one plant after another
newly planted,

your face
stained
by a kiss
of mud,
you go out
and return
flourishing,
you go out
and from your hand
the stem
of the alstromeria
raises its elegant solitude,
the jasmine
graces
the mist of your forehead
with stars of perfume and the dew.

All of you grew, penetrating
into the earth,
and made
immediate
green light,
foliage and power.
You communicated with
your seeds,
my love,
ruby gardener:
your hand
your self
with the earth
and suddenly the clear

growth of a garden.

Love, so too
your hand
of water,
your heart of earth
gave
fertility
and strength to my song.
You touched
my breast
while I slept
and the trees budded
in my dreams.
I woke up, opened my eyes,
and you had planted
inside of me
astonishing stars
that rise
with my song.

So it is, gardener:
our love
is
of the earth:
your mouth is a plant of light, a corolla,
my heart works in the roots.

THE PORTRAIT IN THE ROCK

Yes, I knew him, I lived years
with him, with his substance of gold and stone.
He was a man who was worn down.
In Paraguay he left his father and mother,
his sons, his nephews,
his latest in-laws,
his gate, his hens
and some half-opened books.
They called him to the door.
When he opened it, the police took him
and they beat him up so much
that he spat blood in France, in Denmark,
in Spain, in Italy, traveling,
and so he died and I stopped seeing his face,
stopped hearing his profound silence.
Then once, on a stormy night,
with snow weaving
a pure coat on the mountains,
a horse, there, in the distance,
I looked and there was my friend:
his face was formed in stone,
his profile defied the wild weather,
in his nose the wind was muffling
the howls of the persecuted.
There the man driven from his land returned:
here in his country, he lives, transformed into stone.

HOUSE

Perhaps this is the house I lived in
when neither I nor earth existed,
when all was moon or stone or darkness,
when still light was unborn.
Perhaps then this stone was
my house, my windows or my eyes.
This rose of granite reminds me
of something that dwelled in me or I in it,
a cave, or cosmic head of dreams,
cup or castle, ship or birth.
I touch the stubborn spirit of rock,
its rampart pounds in the brine,
and my flaws remain here,
sprinkled essence that rose
from the depths to my soul,
and stone I was, stone I will be. Because of this
I touch this stone, and for me it hasn't died:
it's what I was, what I will be, resting
from a struggle long as time.

THE NAMES

I didn't write them on the roof-beams because they were famous, but because they were companions.

Rojas Gimenez, the nomad, nocturnal, pierced with the grief of farewells, dead with joy, pigeon breeder, madman of the shadows.

Joaquin Cifuentes, whose verses rolled like stones in the river.

Federico, who made me laugh like no one else could and who put us all in mourning for a century.

Paul Eluard, whose forget-me-not color eyes are as sky blue as always and retain their blue strength under the earth.

Miguel Hernandez, whistling to me like a nightingale from the trees on Princesa Street until they caged my nightingale.

Nazim, noisy bard, brave gentleman, friend.

Why did they leave so soon? Their names will not slip down from the rafters. Each one of them was a victory. Together they were the sum of my light. Now, a small anthology of my sorrows.

I WILL RETURN

Some other time, man or woman, traveler,
later, when I am not alive,
look here, look for me
between the stone and ocean,
in the light storming
through the foam.
Look here, look for me,
for here I will return, without saying a thing,
without voice, without mouth, pure,
here I will return to be the churning
of the water, of
its unbroken heart,
here, I will be discovered and lost:
here, I will, perhaps, be stone and silence.

Poems of Juan Ramon Jimenez
DUSK

Dusk. Great clouds smother the village.
The streetlights are sad and drowsy.
And the yellow moon wanders
            between water and wind.

An odor rises from the drenched countryside.
A greenish star appears behind
            the old bell tower.
The seven o'clock coach passes . . . Dogs bark . . .

Going out on the road I feel the cold moon
on my face . . . near the white cemetery
on the hill, the tall black pines weep.

I wish that all my poems
could be like the sky at night.
The truth of the moment, without history.

That, like the sky, they would yield at every
      moment all things,
with all their stars.
Not childhood, or youth, or age could rob them
or cast a spell on their immense beauty.

A tremor, a flash, the music present and total.
The tremor, the flash, the music in my head,
the sky in my heart. The naked book!

SKY

I had forgotten you,
sky, and you were nothing
more than a vague existence of light,
seen without name,
by my weary, lazy eyes.
And you would appear, among the idle
discouraged words of the traveler,
like a series of tiny lagoons
seen in a watery landscape of dreams. . .

Today I gazed at you slowly,
and you are rising as high as your name.

Sleep is like a bridge
that stretches from today to tomorrow.
Underneath, like a dream,
water flows.

I am like a distracted child,
who they drag by the hand
through the fiesta of the world.

My eyes cling, sadly
to things. . .

And what sorrow when they tear me away!

Don't run, go slow
it is only into yourself
        that you must go!

Go slow, don't run
for the child of yourself, just born
eternal
cannot follow!

Intelligence, give me
the exact name of things!
. . .Let my word be
the thing itself,
newly created again by my soul.
So all those who don't know them
can go through me, to things;
so all those who have already forgotten them,
can go through me, to things;
so all those who love them,
can go through me, to things. . .
Intelligence, give me
the exact name, and your name,
and theirs and mine, for things!

Some Notes On The Poems

"In writing an original poem we are translating the world, transmuting it. Everything we do is a translation, and all translations are in a way creations... the poet is... the universal translator."

-Octavio Paz

Octavio Paz succinctly states the role of the poet as a translator of the world into words (with thanks to fellow poet/translator Alastair Reid who brought Paz's words to my attention). The poems included here traverse the decades of the seventies and eighties and are arranged largely thematically rather than chronologically. Except for a few minor revisions the poems stand as they were written.

I have been translating poetry from the Spanish and Japanese sporadically almost as long as I have been writing it and have included a few samples of each here. A translator is a midwife of the language whose seemingly impossible task it is to recreate a poem from one language to another, and in doing so to create a poem that sounds as if it were written in English. I hope my efforts suceed at that.

The book is divided into seven sections:

Section I contains work from *Rimrock*, *Return*, and uncollected poems focused around the Alleghany National Forest in northern Pennsylvania.

Section II contains the *Pine Hut Poems*, a sequence which reverberates the seasonal cycles and compression of Japanese verse.

Section III contains poems from *I Learn Only To Be Contented* which reflect a four month stay in Kyoto, Japan.

Sections IV and V contain previously uncollected poems.

Section VI contains a few poems from *Rimrock* and *Return* but mainly uncollected material.

Section VII contains previously published translations from a number of books. Special thanks to Hide Oshiro, who is my co-translator from the Japanese, and to Clark Zlotchew, who provided rough English versions for a few of the Spanish poems.

Parts of sections I, II, and VI were published in Japan in *Sitting In Circles*, a bi-lingual English-Japanese collection of my work with translations into Japanese by Yusuke Keida.

My friend, the late poet Joel Oppenheimer, was fond of quoting the French painter Delacroix who said:

"If you're a poet when you are twenty
it's because you are twenty;
if you're a poet when you are forty,
it's because you're a poet"